Travis I. Sivart

27 Thoughts on Cigar Smoking

Travis I. Sivart

Travis I. Sivart

27 Thoughts on Cigar Smoking

Cover Design by Travis I. Sivart
Edited by Tara Moeller

ISBN:

Talk of the Tavern Publishing Group

Travis I. Sivart

Enjoying what you're reading?
Want more? Sign up for Travis's newsletter
and get a free book.

Go to TravisSivart.com and click on the
newsletter link on the menu bar!

Travis I. Sivart

Dedication

This book is an introduction to centuries old hobby and a community of hard-working men and women, who have built an industry that lets an everyday schlep like myself feel a little bit privileged and fancy.

Travis I. Sivart

Contents

27 Thoughts on Cigar Smoking

Travis I. Sivart

Introduction

Welcome to an easy, relaxed, unjudgemental guide to cigar smoking. This book is not every tidbit of information ever given about cigar smoking. It's a reasonable primer for enjoying cigars. It's filled with information about the basics, and you can pick and choose what you like. I guess it's sorta like those "Choose Your Own Adventure" books from the 1980s, except for adults, and includes smoking cigars. Other than that, they're exactly alike!

Each thought is complete on its own, but many tie together and support the others. They're great launching points into further knowledge, or just enough to be a conversation starter at your local cigar lounge.

A few quick things about the terminology; cigars may be called smokes, sticks, and a few other things. The end that you light is called the foot, the end you put in your mouth is called the cap. The leaves on the outside are the wrapper, and the tobacco inside is the filler. There's plenty of other jargon, but that gives you a starting point.

No matter what anyone says, here's the most important rule of enjoying smoking cigars: "Smoke what you like, like what you smoke." Basically, if you're enjoying it, you're doing it right.

I have information on the same topics—as well as other topics—on my live stream, YouTube channel, TikTok, and more. You can find all these and more at TravisSivart.com.

27 Thoughts on Cigar Smoking

1. Your First Cigar

Your first cigar can either be an amazing experience, or a horrid one. There's a slight chance it might be somewhere in between, but usually it's one or the other.

First point of advice, don't inhale. I mean, you *can* inhale, and some folks do. Don't inhale. I've known a couple people who inhale, and I've known a couple people who think they'll be fine inhaling. The second type usually ends up feeling pretty lousy, and the first type are just stubborn. Inhale if you want, but really…don't inhale.

For your first cigar—and by that, I mean your first cigar bought in a cigar store, rather than from behind a gas station counter—I recommend starting with a low to a medium-bodied, medium-flavored cigar. That's a reasonable gauge, so you'll know if you like it, and what direction to move towards for your next cigar if you enjoyed the experience.

I also recommend a shorter cigar, but not too thin. I say this because a thicker cigar has more body and umph to it, and gives you more of the experience. But avoid the seven-inch Churchill for your first smoke. It's almost always too much for a first time smoker.

Ask for advice from experienced smokers, but tell them it'll be your first, so be gentle. They may good-naturedly tease you a bit, but they'll understand and help. We want more people in the hobby, and we're happy to share our thoughts and experiences.

Travis I. Sivart

2. Cutting

After removing the cellophane (if your cigar has cellophane) cutting your cigar is the first thing you do. I'll discuss cutters later—including bullet cutters or punches, v-cutters, pocket knives, teeth, and more—but here's the basics of using a straight cutter.

When cutting your cigar, you want to take the very end off the cap. That's the smooth, rounded part opposite of the flat part you light. Some folks cut a half-inch or more, but I prefer to lay my straight cutter—or guillotine—on a flat surface, set the cap inside the circle of the cutter, and then snap it shut with a quick, clean motion. This will cut off the perfect amount without losing any extra.

If you can't set it on a flat surface, then hold your cutter in one hand, thumb and middle finger in the ends, and insert the cap of the cigar into the open center with the other. Make sure only a little is poking through, and it's lined up straight. Watch your fingers, and snap the two sides of the guillotine together.

It doesn't have to be perfect, but you really should try to avoid doing a hack job of it. Make sure there's no loose tobacco sticking out of the cut, then prepare for lighting your cigar.

Travis I. Sivart

3. Lighting

There's a bit of discussion to be had about lighting a cigar. Some folks feel you should "toast" or "roast" the foot (the end) of the cigar. This is the process of rolling a flame across the end of the cigar, while turning the stick in the fingers of your other hand, causing whole foot to be exposed to the flame and becoming well-charred or even totally lit... all before you put it in your mouth.

Some use matches, others use a butane torch lighter, and some folks prefer to light a strip of cedar and use that bit of flaming wood to do the job. These preferences are largely based on what they find best suits their palate and how it affects the flavor for them.

Other people just pop it in their mouth, light the stick, and puff until the end is glowing and lots of smoke is billowing into the air. You do you, chum, and don't worry about others.

But no matter the method of lighting your cigar, take the time to roll the cigar to light it evenly. This makes an even burn more likely, and an even burn makes for a better smoke.

If you plan to relight a partially smoked cigar, let it go out, knock the remaining ash off the end, blow through its length a few times, then go about your day. When relighting it, blow through it a couple of times before doing so. Between the stale char on one end, and dried saliva on the other end, the cigar won't taste as good as the first time. But this technique will help it taste slightly less ashy and burnt.

Travis I. Sivart

4. Lighters vs. Matches

When lighting a cigar, you can always use what you know. Lighters work fine. From cheap butane Bic lighters, to butane torch lighters, to Zippo naphtha lighters. Or you can use matches, or fancier methods, such as cedar.

The issue some folks have with lighters is they feel the lighter fluid leaves a chemical taste during the lighting, thus tainting their smoking experience. Many say using matches is a cleaner and more pure flavor and experience. I'd ask about the scent and taste of sulphur from the matches, but I don't think anyone considers that an issue. And people aren't wrong. I definitely taste a difference with a Zippo versus other forms of lighting. But it's really is up to the individual tastes and preferences of the smoker.

One more way some folks like to light their cigars is by lighting a strip of cedar on fire and using it to light their cigar. They feel this contaminates the flavor the least, and the natural wood and flavor of the cedar enhances the smoke.

Travis I. Sivart

5. How Low to Go

A lot of folks worry about how low to smoke their cigar, as well as when and how to put it out. They ask if they smoke it to the band, until it burns their fingers, or somewhere in-between.

I smoke my cigars until I can't hold them anymore, whether that's because of the heat or because it's just too small. I choose to do this because I want to get every cent of value out of something I paid for, and not for any better reason.

The flavor of a cigar changes towards the end. Though some cigars change flavor profiles slightly as you smoke them, the change at the end is often because of moisture and saliva buildup from the smoker.

I'll tell you this: smoke it until you're done. Whether that's a few puffs or until your fingertips are hot, as long as you enjoy smoking the cigar, you're doing okay.

As for putting a cigar out; if you're outdoors and throw it on the ground, make sure it's out. No need for forest fires. If you're indoors, such as at a cigar lounge, set it on an ashtray and let it go out naturally. Stubbing a cigar out can cause noxious fumes and upset others as you scamper out the door.

Travis I. Sivart

6. Filler & Binder

Filler is the stuff inside a cigar. Long filler tends to be long and whole leaves used in higher quality cigars. Short filler—ground up or chopped leaves—is used in cheaper cigars.

Binder is the layer between the filler and the wrapper, and it holds the filler together. The filler and the binder together make the inside of a cigar covered by the wrapper. Some companies will use two binder leaves to give an added complexity to a smoke.

Travis I. Sivart

7. Wrappers

Wrappers are the leaves around everything else. This is the feature by which most people judge cigars. A good wrapper enhances the flavor of a cigar and gives it tones such as spicy, peppery, leathery, etc. If a wrapper looks bad, most folks will avoid that cigar. Like judging a book by its cover.

Wrappers:

- Green
    - Double Claro or Candela
    - Mild, grass, cedar, pepper, light sweetness
- Tan
    - Connecticut
    - Mild with woody, spicy, or cedar taste
- Light brown/red
    - Claro
    - Natural, sweeter, cedar, coffee,
- Medium brown—Colorado
    - Corojo, spicy, peppery, robust
    - Criollo, cocoa, cedar, nuts, light sweetness
    - Habano, heavy and spicy
    - Sumatra, mild & sweet with cinnamon zest
- Dark brown
    - Maduro, sweeter, caramel
- Black
    - Oscuro or Double Maduro.

Travis I. Sivart

8. Length

Size makes a difference, doesn't it? I'll discuss thickness in the following chapter, but right now, I want to discuss length. Want to know the dominant difference made by cigar length? Longer cigars last longer. That's about it.

Of course, a longer cigar provides a cooler smoke, but it eventually gets shorter, thus not cooling any more than a cigar of the shorter length.

General cigar sizings, or dimensions, are written out as length by ring gauge. So a 6x40 cigar would be six inches long, and have a 40 ring gauge (5/8th inch diameter).

Travis I. Sivart

9. Ring Gauge

I love a larger ring gauge. It adds to the fullness, richness, and flavor of a cigar. The thicker a cigar, the cooler the smoke. And often a thinner ring gauge means it burns hotter, and may get bitter or harsh near the end of the smoke. Wrappers on smaller cigars will influence the flavor more than on a thicker cigar.

Ring gauge measures the diameter of a cigar in $1/64^{th}$ of an inch increments. So a 40 ring gauge cigar would be $40/64^{th}$ (or $5/8^{th}$) of an inch.

There are no hard and fast rules for sizing, but the industry has a general guideline that most companies stick to.

Size Range of Length in Inches x Ring Gauge:

- **Belicoso**: 6" to 6-1/2" x 48-54
- **Petite Belicoso**: 5" to 5-1/4" x 40-42
- **Churchill**: 6-1/2" to 8" x 47-50
- **Corona**: 5-1/4" to 5 3/4" x42-44
- **Double Corona**: 6-3/4" to 8" x 49-52
- **Gigante, Presidente**: 8" to 10" x 52-64
- **Londsdale**: 6" to 7" x 42-44
- **Panatela**: 6" to 7" x 34-39
- **Petite Corona**: 4-3/4" to 5" x 38-42
- **Robusto**: 5" to 5 3/4" x 48-52
- **Rothschild**: 4-1/2" to 5" x 48-50
- **Toro**: 6" to 6-1/2" x 50-54

10. Strength

Cigar strength ranges from mild (or light) to medium-bodied and full-bodied. And like the steak range (rare, medium, well done) it also has the middle ground between each of those three indicators, and we phrase those as mild to medium bodied, and medium to full-bodied. This is sometimes referred to as the "magnitude" of the cigar, indicating the "oomph" to it.

Mild cigars are less powerful and are often good cigars for a first time smoker to try. Medium is the middle ground, and is a good place to start if you favor bolder flavors in whiskeys, beers, or foods. Full-bodied cigars tend to be too much for many folks, but it's my favorite.

There's also a flavor range. This is the combination of taste and smell, which are inexorably intertwined. Flavor can be drastically different between smokers; some folks tasting nuances and intricacies, while other just know they like it. Don't expect to pick out the different flavors listed in a description right away, or possibly ever. Just know whether or not you like it.

Travis I. Sivart

11. Bands

Many smokers debate whether you should leave a paper cigar band on or remove it when smoking. The former usually says it helps keep the wrapper intact and aids in the cigar's smoking. If you need a band to keep a cigar tight and together, then I'd question the construction of the cigar as a whole.

The latter like to smoke it past where the band becomes an obstruction, without having to worry about removing it while enjoying a stick. Also, sometimes a poorly glued band can cause the tearing of the wrapper, which can lead to it unraveling or otherwise create issues. It's easier to deal with these issues if your smoke isn't lit when doing so.

I like to remove my band. And you can choose to do as you like, and even vary it up. Go wild, leave it on for a touch of mystery, or strip it off and smoke it naked!

Travis I. Sivart

12. Ash

Winston Churchill is a well-known cigar smoker, and there's a great story about him smoking cigars in Parliament. He'd secretly slide a hat pin (a long thin needle the length of a finger) into his cigar so the ash wouldn't fall off. As he smoked his long cigar (a size now known as a Churchill, named after him), and the length of the ash grew to incredible proportions, it would distract Parliament members from whoever was speaking. They were more interested in if his ash would topple off his cigar than what the other person was saying.

The ash of a cigar may indicate the quality of a cigar. A well-constructed cigar will have an ash that doesn't crumble or fall apart at the slightest movement. A loose packed, or poorly constructed, cigar will often drop ash willy-nilly and often in flakes.

Ash can help cool a smoke and help prevent an uneven burn as you smoke. Many folks recommend you leave a small bit of ash on your cigar when possible, and don't constantly tap it off as soon as it forms. Depending on the cigar, knock the ash off when it becomes unstable or loose.

Travis I. Sivart

13. Ashtrays

An odd thing to want to talk about, but an intricate and necessary part of cigar smoking. Enjoying this hobby means you get to collect accouterment that goes with smoking cigars, including ashtrays. Your first should be large enough that you can set your cigar down on the ashtray without risking it rolling off or flipping out.

You can use a standard cigarette ashtray, but remember your cigar burns hotter than a cigarette because of size alone. Cheap or thin ashtrays may crack. Most cigar ashtrays are ceramic or metal to avoid that. I've had a beautiful, custom made 3D printed ashtray in the shape of my podcast logo, with the image on the bottom, and it burned. After a few uses, there were scorch rings on the bottom from cigar tips, so consider the material.

Take a look at the local cigar lounge (not cigar store, that's very different) and see what they're using. Usually they'll have some for sale. If not, then check at some online retailers. I encourage you to get one large enough to hold more than one cigar at a time, because this is a social hobby and you may want to have some friends over to enjoy a smoke, or bring it to the monthly poker game.

Travis I. Sivart

14. Cutters

Cutters—the things we use to snip the tip from our smokes—come in a variety of shapes, colors, and costs. The first thing I'd like to explain is the various cuts; straight, bullet, v-cut, and alternative.

A straight cut, usually using a guillotine cutter, is the most common. You can find these in most stores that have cigars, from cigar lounges, to smoke and vape shops, to places like Walgreens and CVS.

Alternative cuts would be using your pocket knife, teeth, or fingernails. I don't recommend these, but you do what you must do in a pinch. Speaking of pinching, given the choice of biting or using your fingers, I recommend pinching. Stops you from getting a bunch of bits of tobacco in your mouth.

A bullet cutter, also called a punch cutter or a hole cutter, creates a deep hole to pull smoke through. This is my favorite because it focuses the flavor of the cigar.

And that brings us to the V-cutter, also known as a wedge cutter. This is my second favorite cut and is a blend of the above two.

Travis I. Sivart

15. Flavored Cigars

Flavored cigars are a growing market. Some say the largest growth segment in the cigar industry. I know my wife enjoys them more than a "normal" cigar. They're infused with a flavor. Alcohols, coffee, fruits, honey, and more.

This can be done in a variety of ways. One company uses a humidification process for the filler, others are injected, sprayed on the binder, or coated onto the wrapper and, especially, the cap. They range from cheap mass, machine-produced to a few rare hand-rolled cigars.

Once looked down upon, and often still are, they've gained popularity and acceptance in recent years. Some people say flavored cigars often leaves lingering tastes on their palate.

I recommend keeping flavored cigars in a separate humidor to avoid flavor contamination with other unflavored cigars. I like to keep my flavored cigars in glass canning jars, each flavor in its own container.

Travis I. Sivart

16. Cellophane

This is the plastic covering most cigars when you buy them. There's debate if you should leave it on or take it off a cigar before storing it in a humidor. It boils down to personal preference.

Some feel the cellophane helps keep their sticks humidified and assists in aging. Once it has aged a bit, you'll notice the plastic turning yellow as it soaks up the oils from the wrapper. Keeping it on also helps prevent your cigars from taking on the flavor of other cigars in your humidor.

I personally enjoy pulling the cellophane off as part of the ritual of smoking.

Travis I. Sivart

17. Storage & Aging

Humidors are the most common way of storing your cigars. You can buy or make these and often have gadgets like hygrometers to help monitor the humidity in your box.

Proper humidity is essential. The best humidity for cigars is between 65% and 72%. If the humidity is too low, the cigars will burn, but the smoke will have no taste. If the humidity is too high, the cigars can develop mold.

The most common protocol for storing cigars is the 70/70 rule. This rule states that cigars should be kept at 70% humidity and 70 degrees Fahrenheit. Your humidity can vary depending where you live and the humidity levels of your house and region; therefore, it's important to monitor it.

If you're storing cigars for long periods of time, or aging, serious collectors may adjust these levels. For long-term aging, a slightly lower humidity (62-65%) is better. You can use a digital hygrometer to protect your cigar collection.

In regards to aging, letting a cigar rest for months, or even more than a year, can change the flavor. It often mellows a smoke and gives it more complexity as flavors blend. Kinda like next-day lasagna or chili.

Travis I. Sivart

18. Alternative Storage

If a humidor isn't your thing, or if you have too many cigars to fit into the humidors you have, then you have options. Many people use DIY storage containers. From glass canning jars, to plastic totes of various sizes, to coolers (often referred to as coolidors) set up for long-term storage, and more.

The trick is to make sure you keep each of them at the proper humidity level. Each should have their own hygrometer and humidity packs. I prefer using canning jars with mesh lids, filled with water gel beads to keep things level. A quick internet search will get you enough ideas that you could write an entire book about it.

Travis I. Sivart

19. Humidor Care

It's important to keep your humidor properly maintained. You should monitor the humidity weekly to get a feel for how often you need to refresh your humidity packs or whatever. Some places you need to do it more often, others less often.

When you first get a humidor and before you load it with cigars, you'll need to condition it by rubbing it down with distilled water. It's important to use distilled water in particular since it's had the minerals removed. Minerals in your water can clog the cedar and hamper the humidification process. You should wipe it down so the inside is moist but not dripping, allowing the wood to absorb the moisture. Otherwise, the humidor will suck all the humidity up and leave nothing for your cigars.

How often should you repeat this? As needed, or when you notice it's not maintaining the humidity level you need.

20. Refilling a Torch Lighter

This may sound simple to some, and a complete mystery to others. It's easy once you know what you're doing.

Use butane fuel specifically for a torch lighter. Quality matters here and I recommend using a name brand like Zippo. Make sure it's not Zippo naphtha lighter fluid, that's just for the flip top lighters with cotton and a flint. Cheaper fuels can gum up the nozzle and cause clogging.

Flip your lighter upside down and check the bottom for the place to stick your butane fuel. It's a little hole, often with the flame height adjuster around it. Insert the butane nozzle and push gently but firmly. You should hear a little hiss. Do this a few times. If you have a fuel window, watch it until it's full.

That's it. Nice and easy. Sometimes it's necessary to "bleed" your lighter as it fills with propellant and doesn't leave any room for the flammable accelerant gas. To clear it out, just use a safety pin, a paperclip, a pocket knife, or whatever and push on the fill nozzle. Do this with the lighter upright, then upside down, until nothing else comes out. Once it's empty, fill it with butane fluid, as detailed above.

Travis I. Sivart

21. Purchasing Boxes of Cigars

To save money and keep your humidor full, consider purchasing a box (or boxes) of cigars. This often saves you a nice chunk of change. Most cigars come in a box of twenty, though some contain eighteen or even thirty. When purchasing a box, it usually saves you at least ten percent, but usually much more than that.

I guess this is a good place to mention samplers. Samplers are an assortment of cigars ranging from five to many more, even up to dozens bundled together, called bundles, oddly enough. It's a great way to try a variety without breaking the bank.

Travis I. Sivart

22. Cigar Retailers

Let's talk about where to buy cigars. At the time of writing this book, there are smoke shops, which have vaping supplies but often have a small selection of cigars. A few dozen brands in various sizes can be found in a glass-fronted humidified cabinet.

But if you can find a local cigar lounge, they'll have a much larger selection and you can sit with other cigar smokers in leather chairs with televisions around the room to enjoy your purchase. I urge you to shop a cigar lounge if you have one within a reasonable range of your stomping grounds; it's worth it.

Another option is shopping online. Huge cigar retailers exist on the web, and that's the place to go for a wide selection of samplers, boxes, and individual smokes. The actual choice here is paying a little more to support a local business, or saving money by shopping online.

Either way, once you have your purchase and get it home, let it "rest" in your humidor. Allowing your new cigars to rest in your humidor for a month or so will make sure they're properly humidified and give you a better smoking experience.

Of course, some of us (I'm pointing at myself) often don't have that kind of patience.

23. Developing Your Palate

When you first begin your journey into the world of cigars, you probably want to begin with mild (aka lighter) cigars. Build your way up to stronger smokes, and stop where you find the most enjoyment.

If you tend to enjoy stronger flavors, you may want to move to medium or full-bodied cigars sooner. For example, if you take your coffee black or like espresso, if you like stout beers over IPAs, if you prefer a strong bourbon over rum...you may prefer a stronger cigar.

Of course, this is all individual preference. Some folks who love lighter flavors in most things, like strong cigars, and others who only drink whiskey straight and black coffee, gravitate to mild cigars. Enjoy experimenting and experiencing the world of cigars until you find what you like. But, in a couple of years, try the full range again. Our tastes can shift and change.

I also find I prefer a heavier cigar later in the day, and a milder one early. Or if I just finished a good steak and baked potato, I want something with a full-body and full flavor afterwards. But I'll get into cigar pairing next.

Travis I. Sivart

24. Cigar Pairings

I feel I must reiterate here that all of this is set by your own preference. Pairing a cigar with the right drink or meal is a wonderful thing, and there are generalizations I'll make here, but in the end, it's you who decides what works best for you. You can also go down the rabbit hole of researching online what sort of smoke goes best with wine or whiskey, steak or fish, and so on.

Okay, a good rule of thumb is heavy with heavy, light with light. For example, if it's fish and linguine, then afterwards a mild cigar and a white wine. If it's barbequing on the grill with sausage, ribs, and burgers, then a medium body and flavor cigar and a beer go well with it. And a steak and potato may call for full-bodied smoke with a nice well-rounded bourbon.

I'm going to leave you with the basic bones of the concept, and suggest you research for more information. So many people will say different things about this. I couldn't fit it into a book by itself, let alone a one-page, one-thought format like this series.

25. Where to Smoke

As time marches on, there are fewer and fewer places we can enjoy a cigar. There are still cigar lounges and a few restaurants that allow it. Here in Richmond, Virginia, we have a wonderful cigar bar that has a humidor, a full menu, and piano bar, and more. You can get a full meal, a drink, and a smoke all in the same place.

In your own home, I recommend smoking in a well-ventilated area. Also, keep in mind, if you smoke in your house, cigar smoke gets into things. Your furniture and curtains will hold the smell, as will any jackets or clothing in the room where you smoke. Just something to be aware of.

Nowadays, even public parks and outdoor areas often have restrictions on smoking. Make sure you check on the local ordinances and rules before lighting up.

26. Reviews

You can find new cigar choices and recommendations by asking others, but you can also find a wealth of helpful advice by reading reviews. There are websites—from retailers to cigar industry publications—that have hundreds of reviews on thousands of cigars. There are cigar magazines, yearly ratings published, and so much more. Just look around and you'll find things everywhere, telling you what cigar to buy next and why.

Remember, though, reviews are just opinions. And opinions are like...well, you know the rest. If you love a cigar and every other review says differently, it doesn't mean you're wrong. And the opposite is true, as well. People love Davidoff, but I'm not a fan. Most of their sticks are just too mild and bland for me, though there are some exceptions. Cohiba? That's like Hollywood's favorite stick! But it isn't even in my top twenty. My point is, everyone has different tastes, and don't follow the crowd just to be in the crowd. Go ahead and stand out.

Speaking of which, remember to leave a review to help others and your favorite cigar retailer. You can do this on social media, cigar sites, and tons of other places. You can also leave a review of this book to help the next newbie cigar smoker decide if it's for them.

Travis I. Sivart

27. Cigar Culture

Cigar smoking is much more than taking in nicotine. It's a ritual and ceremony. It's taking time out from your busy schedule to consciously relax and unwind. It's enjoying your collection of lighters, cutters, ashtrays, and cigars.

It's also about the camaraderie and community. One thing I've learned over decades of enjoying this hobby is that you'll meet a lot of intelligent and opinionated folk. It's a great way to trade thoughts and ideas with people from all walks of life. Cigar lounges are especially good for this.

But I've also had cigar meetups at restaurants, parks, and even science-fiction and fantasy conventions. It can be a solitary activity, or can include socialization that is on a level I've experienced nowhere else.

Travis I. Sivart

About the Author

Travis I. Sivart is a prolific author of Fantasy, Science Fiction, Social DIY, and more. He's created The Traverse Reality, a shared universe that connects his cyberpunk, fantasy, and steampunk worlds, with characters readers love.

Travis I. Sivart has been writing and telling stories since he was a young child. Perhaps it was inevitable he would call grappling with words and language a career—and loving every moment. He's privileged to share his work with a large and welcoming audience. Get in touch to discover more about his work, writing process, and future endeavors.

You can sometimes find him live-streaming the writing and editing of his latest project from his home in Central Virginia, surrounded by too many cats.

You can get a free book, and discover Travis's other series, podcasts, live-streams, social media, and more at www.TravisSivart.com.

Travis I. Sivart

If you enjoyed this book...

Please let others know by reviewing it on Amazon or Goodreads, and let others know your thoughts!

Other books by Travis I. Sivart:

The Portals Series
What if you died and woke up in a new world and in a new body? Three strangers from our world awaken in a world of spells, dragons, and elves in the aftermath of an apocalypse.

The Silver & Smith Chronicles
Silver, a billionaire bounty hunter, joins forces with Henrietta "Hank" Smith to find mystical artifacts in a race against criminals and corporations in a dystopian, cyberpunk world with a dash of pulp noir. Join their ongoing adventures of cyberpulp!

Journal of a Stranger, Volume I & II
The thoughts, ideas, philosophies, and inspirations of a time traveling adventurer. Delving into the psychology of man, life's eternal questions, burning passions, and the quirky pseudo-science of his mind, and more.

The Downfall Series: Harbinger
The Talisman came again, but this time it didn't leave. The magical emanations of the comet have brought terrors from the bowels of the earth and increased the powers of an insane necromancer. The chaos above brought out others seeking to wrest control of the land. Five people from different walks of life are thrown together by these events with the knowledge that the world as they know it is ending.

Travis I. Sivart

27 Thoughts on Cigar Smoking

Travis I. Sivart